HAIL MARY AND RHYTHMIC BREATHING

A New Way of Praying the Rosary

Richard Galentino

Paulist Press
New York/Mahwah, N.J.

Cover design by Cynthia Dunne
Book design by Lynn Else

Library of Congress Cataloging-in-Publication Data

Galentino, Richard.
    Hail Mary and rhythmic breathing : a new way of praying the rosary / Richard Galentino.
        p. cm.
    Includes bibliographical references.
    ISBN 0-8091-4339-9 (alk. paper)
    1. Rosary. 2. Breathing exercises. 3. Respiration—Religious aspects—Christianity. 4. Meditation. I. Title.

    BX2310.R7G33 2005
    242'.74—dc22

                                                                2005001957

Published by Paulist Press
997 Macarthur Boulevard
Mahwah, New Jersey 07430

www.paulistpress.com

Printed and bound in the
United States of America

Contents

To my Mom

You must be the change you wish to see in the world.
—Mahatma Gandhi

Reflection from a Roman Catholic Priest

By the incarnation, God entered into human life and the elements of human life became sacred. Jesus shared meals with his disciples and friends, and, as they nourished their bodies, his teaching nourished their minds. So sharing a meal has become a way of developing the Christian faith. Before Jesus left his disciples, he wanted to share another meal with them. There he consecrated bread and wine to become his body and blood. And the meal became sacred in a special way. When he returned to them as the risen Lord, he breathed on them and gave them the power to forgive sins. His breathing on them was a way of sharing God's life with them—for who but God can forgive sin?

Both eating and breathing bring us to the fundamental realities of our life. The Christian tradition acknowledges the sacred character of the meal by continuing the

Eucharist, but breathing has not played a significant role in the spiritualities of the West (although synchronized breathing with prayer was proposed in the *Spiritual Exercises of St. Ignatius*).

Thus Eastern traditions have made much of the role of breathing in prayer—a practice that until recently went unrecognized in the West.

Today many in the West have become aware of the yoga and meditation practices of the East. One of these is Richard Galentino. He came from a family that valued the rosary and as a boy he served daily Mass. While continuing his devotions at Georgetown University, he developed an interest in yoga and found it a great help to concentration; here he also learned of Ignatian methods of prayer. Now he is directing Catholic Volunteers in Florida, a program that has people living together while doing a year of community service and faith formation. His devotion to Mary continued for the next eight years as did his interest in yoga. He began finding that yoga exercises helped his Christian prayer and they seemed to belong together.

After practicing the exercises described here for more than a year, Mr. Galentino wrote this guide for others. In the process he has shown how the wisdom of the East can nourish the Christian life. His text can serve as a great source for prayer for the many Christians hoping to deepen their prayer.

Thomas M. King, SJ
Department of Theology
Georgetown University

Reflection from a Yogi

Three well-known Benedictine monks of the Catholic tradition are wonderful examples of the benefits of yoga. Jean-Marie de Cheney, OSB, has written a book, *10 Lessons in Yoga,* in which he encourages his fellow brothers and sisters to take up this practice, which has greatly enhanced his own spirituality. Until his passing several years ago, Father Bede Griffiths, OSB, ran an ashram in India where yoga was practiced along with Mass and all the Catholic rites. His predecessor, also a Benedictine monk and the founder of the ashram, was addressed as *Swamiji* because of his intense yoga spiritual practice on the Arunachala mountain. Father Joe Pereyra, a Jesuit priest residing in Calcutta, worked closely with Mother Teresa teaching yoga to the AIDS patients. He is still continuing with this labor of love.

Richard Galentino seems to be following in the steps of these great souls. He is opening up the possibility that Catholic practitioners can benefit from one of the wonderful tools of the system of yoga. With this present work, Richard beautifully intersperses the devotional practice of the prayer to the Blessed Virgin Mary with the conventional practice of yoga called *pranayama*.

Pranayama is the fourth limb in the system compiled by Maharishi Patanjali, called Raja Yoga or "kingly" yoga. The eight limbs of this system are: *yamas* and *niyamas*, ethical principles; *asanas*, postures; *pranayama*, breathing exercises; *pratyahara*, control of the senses; *dharana*, concentration; *dhyana*, meditation; and *samadhi*, superconsciousness. The practice of *pranayama* is considered key to the whole system.

Prana is a Sanskrit word and, as is the case with most Sanskrit words, it has many different meanings depending on the context in which it is used. But in the context we are using it, it is made up of two syllables: *ana*, which means "the smallest thing that has ever existed," and *pra*, which means "that which existed before anything else." This eternal element gives it a divine quality. It is considered to be the life force: that which keeps the human being alive. Some people call it electricity. *Prana* is mainly brought into our bodies through our breath and is often equated to air but that is not entirely accurate. In the same way that sound waves or radio waves carry the music from a station to the receiver, the air carries the *prana* or life force. Breathing exercises are considered one of the main methods of manipulating or working with the *prana*; thus *pranayama* means the control of *prana*.

  Prana has often been equated with the Holy Spirit. It is not uncommon in the practice of yoga to see the divine or the spiritual intertwined with the more physical aspects or more earthly activities. It is marvelous to see how the practice of *pranayama* leads to the control of the senses, those unruly advisors that get us into so much trouble. Having those senses under control makes it easier to concentrate, and concentration is the door to meditation. Through meditation, the stillness of the movement of the mind allows us to step into the spiritual world where angels, archangels, virtues, and powers are glorifying God incessantly. The practice of *pranayama* is one of the many tools which yoga offers to help us to deal with our physical limitations and mental defilements that are so difficult to overcome when sincere efforts are made to seek union with God.

  At this critical time, when personal spiritual practice is one way that we can help bring peace to this troubled world, Richard has skillfully incorporated this valuable tool of *pranayama* with a devotional practice to the Blessed Virgin Mary. The meditations around the Hail Mary provide a wonderful framework for a truly meaningful devotional practice. The devotion to the Blessed Virgin Mary is capable of reaching the heart of any human being as a reflection of her own relationship with the One who brought him into this world. Therefore, the potential to share this valuable gift of *pranayama* to increase the spiritual growth of those seeking to come closer to God is crystallized through this book. I would like to encourage the readers to practice it faithfully and to trust that wonderful results will be forthcoming, and, with the help of the Blessed Virgin Mary, that peace will prevail.

Victor (Vyasa) Landa
Shanti Yoga Center for Harmony
4217 East-West Highway
Bethesda, MD 20814
E-mail: Shantiyoga@schooloflife.org
www.schooloflife.org

Introduction

*S*ince 1996, meditation, prayer, and yoga have been a part of my life. Sometimes they are a part of my daily routine and sometimes I am struggling to make them a part of my daily routine. I have always desired to make meditation, prayer, and yoga an integral part of my life, as natural as brushing my teeth, but have not always been successful. I feel that there is great wisdom in the time and effort that Mother Teresa and Mahatma Gandhi put into meditation and prayer. To them, meditation and prayer became a natural part of their morning routine and a supernatural source of energy propelling their great undertakings. Quiet time alone in conversation with God helped them connect *their actions with the will of God, and, as a result, they acted humbly with authority.*

In my meditation during the 2002 Advent season I found myself silently saying the Hail Mary. I had never really concentrated or put effort into praying the Hail Mary. I knew the prayer well, as most Catholics do. I remember as a boy having to pray three Hail Marys as penance after the sacrament of reconciliation, and listening to the fifteen decades of the rosary in procession as an altar boy at May crowning. Now, as an adult, I find myself continually going back to the Hail Mary in my hour of daily meditation. In particular, I find myself coordinating my breath with the three parts of the Hail Mary. The peace of mind and body resulting from meditatively breathing through the Hail Mary has then allowed me to better enter into a conversation with our Mother, Jesus, and God the Father. In this book I share with you the art of yoga breathing, *pranayama,* combined with the grace of the Hail Mary.

Before meditating, place yourself in a prayerful position that will aid your breathing. One of the many yoga positions *(asanas)* is very helpful. Sitting positions that are excellent for meditation include easy pose (sitting with your legs crossed, Indian style), half-lotus, lotus, kneeling, and kneeling with your buttocks on your heels.[1] If none of these positions is comfortable for you, sit in a straight-backed chair or rocking chair. Meditation also works well in many of the different, more advanced yoga positions *(asanas)*, and assists the body in maintaining flexibility and vitality.

Inhale

Hail Mary,
full of grace,
the Lord is with thee.

W*hile inhaling deeply and being conscious of your breath, silently pray: "Hail Mary, full of grace, the Lord is with thee."*

Breath is life.[2] Our first breath at birth gives life to our body. Without food, water, or sunlight, we can exist for days, but without breath we soon die. In today's society of cell phones, e-mails, pagers, and instant messaging we are busier than ever. In our busyness, many of us have forgotten how to breathe properly. Indeed, the only people who seem to take time to breathe are smokers. Ten-minute breaks are routine among smokers as they congregate outside buildings to breathe and talk. Unfortunately, they are breathing polluted air. If breath is fundamental to our physical well-being, we should not take it for granted. Yoga masters from antiquity realized the importance of proper breathing and created the art of breath control, *pranayama*.[3] Proper breathing helps bring more oxygen to our body and helps calm and focus the mind for meditation and conversation with God. Every breath is God's gift of life to us.

Proper inhalation requires retraining the body to breathe through the nose and fully use the capacity of our lungs. We breathe nasally to warm and clean the air before it passes the larynx and trachea en route to the lungs.

Yoga teaches that by breathing nasally we are able to absorb *prana*, life force, or what I prefer to call the grace of God. *Prana* is brought into our central nervous system and brain through the olfactory organs at the back of the nose.[4] Each breath becomes a prayer in which we inhale God's energy and grace through the air.

Inhale; expand the abdomen. As your abdomen and rib cage expand, your diaphragm and chest also move, massaging the internal abdominal organs.[5] By expanding the lungs fully, we also fill all of the air sacs in our lungs, the alveoli, increasing our energy. Without deep breathing, the air sacs at the bottom of our lungs die or become weakened and our physical energy diminishes. People who live in areas of much air pollution also suffer from diminished energy because of the destruction of these air sacs. Inhale deeply in clean air.

Life lived well is a prayer. As breathing gives life to our body, prayer gives life to our soul. The Hail Mary through repetition can breathe life into our soul and prepare us for a conversation with God the Father, Jesus, or Mary.

In meditation, coordinate your inhalation while silently praying, "Hail Mary, full of grace, the Lord is with thee." The angel Gabriel certainly did not want to startle Mary of Nazareth and so he greeted her with these kind words, reminding her that she was full of God's grace (Luke 1:26-38). Imagine Gabriel instructing Mary to take a deep breath and relax, as he needed to have a conversation with her on behalf of God. Similarly, before a test or challenging situation, we often ask a student or friend to sit down and take a deep breath. Unconsciously, we are inviting that person to breathe in God deeply, utilizing God's grace, *prana*, found in each breath of air. Then we can better meet the challenge we face. Just as God was *with* Mary and showed her divine favor, God shows *us* favor.

While silently repeating the first part of the Hail Mary as we inhale, we are also practicing *japa yoga*, which is mental repetitive prayer. Repetitive prayer has been a practice of all major religions since antiquity to help clear the mind and focus it on God. To assist with this prayer practice we often use a rosary to tally the number of Hail Marys we offer. The use of prayer beads is common to Hinduism and Islam as well as to Christianity. In fact, prayer beads are mentioned in Hindu spiritual writings as early as 800 BC.

Buddhists and Hindus both commonly use 108 beads in their prayer strands. Muslims use prayer strands with 99 beads, one each for the 99 names or attributes of Allah. The origin of the rosary is a mystery. The *Catechism of the Catholic Church* says medieval piety in the Western Church developed the prayer of the rosary as a popular substitute for the Liturgy of the Hours. Another theory suggests the rosary was developed by Crusaders who adopted Muslim prayer beads to Christianity. Fifty beads tallying 50 Hail Marys to be repeated three times to total 150 offerings became standard practice. Some theologians suggest that the number 150 reflects the 150 psalms of David, recitation of which was a common part of ninth-century monastic life. Regardless of the origin of the rosary and the number of beads on different prayer strands, the spiritual and health benefits of repetitive prayer have been known for ages by mystics—facts now being supported by Western research.

Researchers are continuing to study the effect of the rosary and mantras.[6] In the 2001 *British Medical Journal*, scientists reported that repeating the rosary or a mantra decreased the respiration rate to six breaths per minute in participants. The normal breathing rate of these participants was fourteen breaths per minute, or eight breaths per minute when in conversation. Slower respiration has favorable effects on the cardiovascular and respiratory systems.[7] Leading medical schools such as that at Harvard University have created institutes to continue the research on the benefits of meditation and prayer on the heart and other physical organs. Many Catholics, of course, have known these positive effects for years because of their daily devotional practices. Such favorable health benefits are needed in today's society with the rise of blood pressure and stress.

As the Hail Mary has three parts, each breath has three parts. The inhale is followed by the second part, retention of breath, just as Gabriel's visit to Mary is followed by Mary's visit to her cousin, Elizabeth.

Inhaling God's grace, go and share it with another as Mary did with her kinswoman.

Hold Your Breath

Blessed are thou among women,
and blessed is the fruit of thy womb, Jesus.

While holding your breath and being conscious of God's grace, silently pray: "Blessed art thou among women, and blessed is the fruit of thy womb, Jesus."

Retention of breath leads to awareness of our body, mind, and environment. When we make an effort to concentrate one of our senses on a particular point of observation, we naturally suspend or hold our breath to sharpen our awareness. Likewise in meditation, by holding our breath for a controlled period of time, we are able to control the flow of energy into our being. This sharpens the powers of observation, allowing increased life force into our spiritual being and oxygen into our lungs. Controlled retention also helps us *deeply* inhale and exhale.

When we breathe shallowly we do not retain proper life force or oxygen. Similarly in life, we often participate or perform activities without proper focus and retention. Have you ever read a page in a book and, after you turned the page, found you could not remember anything you had read? Today's Western society has an increasing problem with retention and focus. Many households have a member or friend who suffers from attention deficit disorder (ADD). Our society as a whole is becoming increasingly affected by a lack of focus and shortness of attention span, and, as a result, the media and advertising agencies have to use increasingly catchy and shocking ways to market their news and products to us. News programs today on TV often have three streams of messaging: the news person talking, an instant news-alert stream that we can read on the bottom of the screen, and a headline (like "America At War"). Producers are hoping that they can grab our attention through at least one of these multiple streams of messaging. As for retaining information that we watch on TV, maybe it is good that we suffer from poor retention. Nonetheless, retention of breath and information is an increasing challenge for our society.

Retention of breath is the second part of proper breathing and corresponds to the second part of the Hail Mary. Holding your breath, silently pray, "Blessed are thou among women, and blessed is the fruit of thy womb, Jesus." This is the salutation with which Elizabeth greeted her cousin, Mary, as recorded in the Gospel of St. Luke (Luke 1:42). The word "Jesus" was not originally a part of Elizabeth's salutation to Mary as recorded in the Bible but was added to the prayer much later. Some theologians attribute the addition of the word "Jesus" in the Hail Mary to Pope Urban IV (1261-64).[8] Of importance is not the actual date of the change, but that the prayer is evolving with time and the inspirations of the Spirit. From the visit of the angel Gabriel, to Elizabeth's greeting of Mary, to the focus on "Jesus" added in the thirteenth century, the Hail Mary prayer continues to evolve with new understandings given by the Spirit.

Tracing the evolution of the Hail Mary in our church community, we follow Mary's steps to her cousin Elizabeth's home. Feeling God's favor, and having heard that God also blessed Elizabeth with a child, Mary journeyed to the home of her kinswoman. While meditation and prayer can be silently offered to God alone, there is power and joy in community prayer. When researchers studied the effects of mantras and the rosary on their participants, they found that everyone's breathing rate was reduced on average to six breaths per minute.[9] The community of participants breathed and benefited together. Likewise, Mary and Elizabeth aided each other throughout their pregnancies and childbirths.

The power of community prayer is often found as groups of individuals gather to pray the rosary. In Lourdes, France, the rosary is often heard. Groups recite it on their journey to Lourdes in trains and buses and on their walk to the pools and grotto where the sick are carried by volunteers in procession.[10] My brother Peter and I experienced the power of group prayer on our pilgrimage to Lourdes in May, 2003. This community/group spirit is nourishing to the soul. Mother Teresa said that the greatest disease of our time is "the feeling of being unwanted, uncared for and deserted by everybody."[11] Together in the rosary we fight against loneliness and commune with others in meditation. "Esprit de corps" or teamwork helps us as individuals within a community stay focused in prayer.

Our emphasis on individuality in the West denies this "esprit de corps" which we crave as humans. Ironically, an easy way to reconnect to this "esprit de corps" is through community violence, war. Why is there so much war in society? We like it. We like the feeling of community when we are all enduring hardship together and focused on victory.

In 1917 Mary appeared at Fatima (a recognized and approved apparition of Mary by the Roman Catholic Church) to combat pending war and pleaded with us to pray the rosary to end war and create peace. Our Mother is suggesting a more difficult but more fruitful way to obtain the "esprit de corps" and community that we often crave as human beings. The path to war, however, is quick and offers immediate excitement to our Western boredom. Meditation with the rosary requires more effort, but the result is peace.

The ability to retain breath helps us increase the discipline that we bring to our activities. While sporadic meditation is better than no meditation, the true benefits of meditation come with discipline and a continued daily practice. I suggest meditating for one hour daily and using the Hail Mary at the beginning of the meditation to help remain focused. The time of day, place, and duration can change, but it is ideal if you can make this a regular part of your daily regimen. The body and mind love routine, especially in today's stressful world. Keeping part of your daily routine sacred will allow you to have a wellspring of energy from which you can draw throughout the day. Both Mother Teresa and Mahatma Gandhi religiously made several hours of meditation and prayer part of their daily routine. Gandhi would spend one or two hours each afternoon meditating at his spinning wheel while spinning up to 40 yards of cloth. At the center of the Indian flag today is a hand spinning wheel, a tribute to Gandhi's emphasis on meditation and self-sufficiency. Mother Teresa spent hours each day in prayer and adoration of the Blessed Sacrament. Time meditating in the presence of God gave Mother Teresa great conviction in her work. With belief in her action, and God on her side, governments and persons who tried to oppose her were humbled. In 1985 Mother Teresa asked Ethiopian officials for two unused buildings to use for orphanages she planned to establish. After initial protests, the officials soon gave in to God's will and Mother Teresa's belief that two orphanages were needed. Mother Teresa also attributed the growth of her religious order of sisters, the Missionaries of Charity, to their order's daily holy hour. Mother Teresa wrote in a message, "In 1963 we were making a weekly holy hour together, but it was not until 1973, when we began our daily holy hour that our community started to grow and blossom."[12] The first half hour Mother Teresa and her sisters prayed the rosary, the second half hour they prayed silently.

Ironically, in today's busy world in which productivity is of paramount importance, we do not have time for proper prayer and meditation. As a result, during the day our energies are dissipated and we do not act with the belief and confidence necessary to be truly productive. Our energies decrease because our actions often are not in line with God's plan. Gandhi and Mother Teresa's attention to prayer and meditation gave them an enormous amount of energy and life force, which spiritualized and gave momentum to their great works. Their actions corresponded with God's plan and this placed the momentum of God behind their works. Gandhi and Mother Teresa forged ahead with Godspeed, changing people's lives. They continue to change many more lives even after their deaths.

Retaining breath, grace is changed and increased within us. Exhaling gives us the opportunity to breathe into the universe.

Exhale

Holy Mary, mother of God,
pray for us sinners,
now and at the hour of our death. Amen.

While exhaling and being conscious of God's grace, silently pray: "Holy Mary, mother of God, pray for us sinners, now and at the hour of our death. Amen."

Exhaling is the most important part of breathing. By exhaling deeply, we rid our bodies of toxins and prepare for proper inhalation. As you exhale, the abdomen contracts and the diaphragm and chest also move, massaging the heart and internal organs. The exhale should be prolonged, deliberate, and slow—at least twice as long as the inhale. As you advance in your practice of breathing, the exhale will become longer and longer. While exhaling deeply and gradually, pray silently, "Holy Mary, mother of

God, pray for us sinners, now and at the hour of our death. Amen."

A prolonged exhale emphasizes the importance of preparation and purification in life. Only with proper preparation are we prepared to act with authority. The two most sacred Christian days are Easter Sunday and Christmas Day. Each of these single days is preceded by long periods of preparation, purification, and anticipation. The period of Advent before Christmas consists of four weeks of preparation as we anticipate receiving a new baby, the Christ child. We have many symbols to help prepare us for this coming, including the use of Advent candles. The lit candle is a good tool to help us prepare a place for daily prayer as well as a guide in meditation. Easter Sunday, celebrating the resurrection of Christ from the dead, is preceded by forty days of Lent. Lent is a period of purification and preparation for rebirth, remembering the forty years that Jewish people wandered in the desert preparing to enter the Holy Land. Candles are important during the Easter season as well. We light the Easter candle or Paschal candle on Holy Saturday, recognizing the coming of Christ, the Light of our lives, through the Resurrection. Celebrating Christmas or Easter without the preparation period minimizes the importance of these events in our lives. In our society we often place much emphasis on the actual day of a big event, such as a wedding, birthday, baptism, Christmas or Easter, without emphasizing the importance of the preparation period and the journey.

The purification of ourselves through the exhale also gives new life and rebirth to the universe. Our exhale and our inner peace through meditation breathe new life and energy into the universe. We are co-creators with God through our prayerful and prolonged exhale. It is natural, then, for the exhale to be twice as long (or at least longer) than the inhale. Allowing the ratio of time for the three parts of your breath (inhale–retention–exhale) to coordinate naturally with the three parts of the Hail Mary will result with the exhale being longer than the inhale. Different schools of *pranayama* and different yoga masters suggest different ratios of time for one's inhalation, retention, and exhalation. For this meditation, I suggest allowing your three-part breath to follow the three-part Hail Mary. As you advance in your lung capacity and discipline, pray the Hail Mary slower and increase the duration of each part of your breath. With practice, you will use thirty seconds or even more time to pray and breathe one Hail Mary. Feel God breathing life into you through energy, *prana,* which is formed and changed in you during the retention of breath. Exhaling gives you the opportunity to release this new, changed breath into the continual formation of the universe. Meditation can help stabilize and give us the emotional energy and grace of God to carry us through the preparation and event, as well as our continual journey. Sustained meditation over a long period of time will build a reserve of God's grace that empowers us to confidently meet our challenges on our journey. Meditation, through the grace we exhale, ripples through the universe and helps provide emotional stability in our world. The exhaling calm of prayer and meditation helps maintain the world in a peaceful balance amidst the want of war in the corrupted mind. Meditating with the Hail Mary is a tool of peace given to us by Mary to help prevent another world war.

The third part of the Hail Mary was not given official recognition by the Church until the sixteenth century, again demonstrating that the Hail Mary is a living prayer, evolving over the course of centuries. As the first two parts of the Hail Mary are salutations, individuals later felt the need of an element of petition to our Mother. St. Bernadine of Siena preached a sermon in 1427 recording the third part of the Hail Mary, which was officially fixed in the Breviary of Pope Pius V in 1568.[13] As Gabriel addressed Mary, now we call upon her in the beginning of our prayer. Calling upon Mary, we ask her to intercede for us, and ask Jesus to help us today in our daily activities as well as on our death day. The Gospel reminds us of the importance of Mary in Jesus' concerns. Like a good son, he listens to his mother. The wedding at Cana reminds us of Mary's intentions and empathy for people when she asked her son to aid the groom by replenishing the wine. Mary can intercede for us as she did for this married couple in the ordinary events and celebrations of our lives.

Mary is also an intercessor for us in our darkest moments. At the foot of the cross on Good Friday, Mary accompanied her son through the agony of the Crucifixion. The pain of a mother as she watches her child die is one of the greatest trials anyone could face. As Mary accompanied her son at his death, so we may ask her and rely on her to accompany us throughout our life challenges and at the hour of our death.

The Hail Mary coordinated with yoga breathing is a beautiful prayer by itself. It helps us become centered on God. Centered in God's presence, we are now ready to take the next step in faith and begin a conversation.

Conversation with God

Conversation with God is the heart of meditation. Saying the rosary in meditation while using the art of yoga breathing clears the mind and body and prepares one to have a conversation with Mary, Jesus or God directly. In life there are many distractions that prevent us from seeing and hearing God's will. Meditation is a practice that helps us center ourselves away from the distractions that we build into our lives. Being centered, we can more easily have a conversation with God. We can be ourselves and not worry about being judged. Speak with God like an old friend with whom you have no secrets.

It's easy to give one hour a day to the TV, and reap the benefits. Imagine giving one hour a day to God, imagine the conversation, the benefits, and what you can learn.

Ten Meditations

Be still and know that I am God.
—Psalm 46:10

*I*n meditation, be conscious of God's presence. If *you feel you are too busy in meditation, worried about saying the Hail Mary, coordinating your* breath or body position...

...just sit quietly in the presence of God.

We need to find God, and he cannot be found in noise and restlessness. God is the friend of silence.
—Mother Teresa

Meditation I

Conversation with a Friend

Time: 20 minutes

Position: Easy pose, sitting with legs crossed (Indian style); support your back against a wall if needed. Easy pose helps strengthen the back and spine and clears the mind. Remember to change the position of the top leg after ten minutes. Substitute other comfortable sitting positions with your back straight.

Environment: Light a candle. Place it four feet in front of you on the floor or on a candleholder at eye level. If in a community, put the candle in the center of the group. Check a watch.

Meditation: Begin with one Hail Mary prayed out loud, whether you are alone or in a group. Silently recite one decade of the rosary (ten Hail Marys) and coordinate each Hail Mary with your breath. After the ten Hail Marys, be conscious of God's presence and begin a conversation with God, telling him about your day or last couple of days. Observe your thoughts. If you feel you are becoming distracted from your conversation with God, refocus by silently saying one or two Hail Marys, coordinating your breath with your prayers. After twenty minutes, thank God and Mary for their time. Conclude with one Hail Mary prayed out loud.

Meditation II (Walking)

Walking with a Friend

Time: 20 minutes

Position: Wearing walking shoes, go for a walk in an environment where you can enjoy God's nature. Walking will help you reduce or maintain weight and is good exercise for the whole body. Check a watch.

Environment: God's nature.

Meditation: Begin with saying one Hail Mary out loud, whether you are alone or with others. Silently say one decade of the rosary (ten Hail Marys) and coordinate each Hail Mary with your breath. With practice you will find that the three parts of your breath and of the Hail Mary will synchronize with a specific foot. Meditational walking can be practiced on much longer walks and lengthening the walk will greatly improve your endurance. After ten Hail Marys, be conscious of God's presence and silently begin a conversation with God, telling him about your day. Observe your thoughts and God's creation around you. If you feel you are becoming distracted from your conversation with God, refocus by silently saying one or two Hail Marys, coordinating your breath, step, and part of the Hail Mary. After twenty minutes, thank God and Mary for their time. Conclude with one Hail Mary prayed out loud.

Meditation III

On the Birth of Jesus

Time: 30 minutes

Position: Easy pose, sitting with legs crossed (Indian style); support your back against a wall if needed. Substitute other comfortable sitting positions with your back straight. If in sitting positions on the floor (i.e., easy pose), change position of left and right legs for balance after about fifteen minutes.

Environment: Light a candle. Place it four feet in front of you on the floor or on a holder at eye level. If in community, put the candle in the center of the group. Play soft meditational music if available. Imagine the environment surrounding the birth of Jesus in the stable at Bethlehem. Check a watch.

Meditation: Begin with one Hail Mary prayed out loud, whether you are alone or in a group. Silently say one decade of the rosary (ten Hail Marys) and coordinate each Hail Mary with your breath. After ten Hail Marys, silently become aware of God's presence. Spend about ten minutes at the stable in Bethlehem. Ask Jesus or Mary any questions you might have. Listen. Observe your thoughts. If you feel you are distracted from your conversation with Mary or Jesus, refocus by silently saying one or two Hail Marys, coordinating your breath. After spending enough time at the birth of Jesus with Mary and Joseph, say ten Hail

Marys silently after switching leg positions if necessary. After thirty minutes, say thank you to Mary and Jesus. Conclude with one Hail Mary prayed out loud.

Meditation IV

On Forgiveness

Time: 30 minutes

Position: Easy pose, sitting with legs crossed (Indian style); support your back against a wall if needed. Substitute other comfortable sitting positions with your back straight.

Environment: This is an excellent meditation for communities in conflict to practice together or individuals seeking reconciliation. Light a candle. Place it four feet in front of you on the floor or on a candleholder at eye level. If in community, put the candle in the center. Check a watch.

Meditation: Begin with one Hail Mary prayed out loud, whether you are alone or in a group. Silently say one decade of the rosary (ten Hail Marys) and coordinate each Hail Mary with your breath. After ten Hail Marys, silently become conscious of God's presence and begin a conversation with God, sharing any sins or failings you have on your mind. Observe your thoughts. If you feel you are distracted from your conversation with God, refocus by silently saying one or two Hail Marys, coordinating your breath. After about ten minutes ask God for forgiveness and express your sorrow. Observe any thoughts or ideas that you might have that would lead you to reconcile yourself in action with a brother or sister. Switch your sitting position if necessary. Pray silently ten Hail Marys. After thirty minutes, thank God and Mary for their time. Conclude with one Hail Mary prayed out loud.

Act: Go and act on any prayerful thoughts you may have had with regard to reconciling yourself with a neighbor, sister, brother, or loved one.

Meditation V

On the Crucifixion

Time: 40 minutes

Position: Easy pose, sitting with legs crossed (Indian style); support your back against a wall if needed. Substitute other comfortable sitting positions with your back straight. Try kneeling with your buttocks resting on your heels.

Environment: Light a candle. Place it four feet in front of you on the floor or on a candleholder at eye level. If in a community, put the candle in the center of the group. Imagine yourself at the foot of the cross as Jesus was being nailed and hung. You are kneeling next to Mary. Check a watch.

Meditation: Begin with one Hail Mary prayed out loud, whether you are alone or in a group. Silently say two decades of the rosary (twenty Hail Marys) and coordinate each Hail Mary with your breath. Imagine yourself at the foot of the cross while saying these Hail Marys, kneeling next to Mary. After twenty Hail Marys, silently become conscious of God's presence and begin a conversation with Jesus, talking to him about his suffering and the suffering and crosses you bear in your life. Observe your thoughts. If you feel you are distracted from your conversation with Jesus, refocus by silently saying one or two Hail Marys, coordinating your breath with your prayer. After twenty minutes, thank Jesus for the gift of his life. Change your seated position if necessary during the meditation. Say two more decades of the rosary silently, kneeling at the foot of the cross next to Mary. Thank Mary and Jesus. Conclude with one Hail Mary prayed out loud.

Meditation VI

On the Resurrection

Time: 40 minutes

Position: Easy pose, sitting with legs crossed (Indian style); support your back against a wall if needed. Substitute other comfortable sitting positions with your back straight. Try kneeling with your buttocks resting on your heels for half the time.

Environment: Light a candle. Place it four feet in front of you on the floor or on a candleholder at eye level. If in community, put the candle in the center of the group. Imagine yourself at the empty tomb on the morning after Jesus rose from the dead. He appears to you as he did to Mary Magdalene in the garden of the tomb on Easter Sunday morning. Check a watch.

Meditation: Begin with one Hail Mary prayed out loud, whether you are alone or in a group. Silently say two decades of the rosary (twenty Hail Marys) and coordinate each Hail Mary with your breath. Imagine yourself in the garden at the empty tomb and the Holy Spirit and Jesus appear to you. After twenty Hail Marys, become aware of God's presence and silently begin a conversation with Jesus, talking to him as you walk through the garden together. Ask Jesus any questions you might have. Observe your thoughts. If you feel you are distracted from your conversation with Jesus, refocus by silently saying one or two Hail Marys, coordinating your breath. After twenty minutes, thank Jesus for his time. Change your seated position if necessary. Say two more decades of the rosary silently while at the empty tomb in the garden. Thank Mary and Jesus. Conclude with one Hail Mary prayed out loud.

Meditation VII

On Life Vocation

Time: 50 minutes

Position: Easy pose, sitting with legs crossed (Indian style); support your back against a wall if needed. Substitute other comfortable sitting positions with your back straight. Try kneeling with your buttocks resting on your heels.

Environment: Light a candle. Place it four feet in front of you on the floor or on a candleholder at eye level. If in a community, put the candle in the center of the group. Check a watch.

Meditation: Begin with one Hail Mary prayed out loud, whether you are alone or in a group. Silently say three decades of the rosary, and coordinate each Hail Mary with your breath. Choose to change your position, *asana*, with each decade of the rosary. After thirty Hail Marys, silently become conscious of God's presence and begin a conversation with Jesus, talking to him about your life and the day-to-day work you do for him. Observe your thoughts and the direction in which you and God want your life to move. If you know yourself truly, your deepest desire will match with the desire of God. In life, we often become distracted and work towards ends that we think are our desires but really are not our truest desire, our God desire. Our energies become dissipated when they are not God's. Talk with God. Search and realize your God desire. Ask God directly, "What do you want me to do?" Listen. If you feel you are distracted from your conversation with God, refocus by silently saying one or two Hail Marys, coordinating the words with your breathing. After thirty minutes, thank God for the gift of life. Change your seated position if necessary. Ask God for the strength and courage to act on your truest desire, your God desire. Say two more decades of the rosary silently. Thank Mary and God. Conclude with one Hail Mary prayed out loud.

Act: Start changing your life's work to match your God desire. If you cannot act on your calling in life, your God desire, continue practicing this meditation until you have the courage to act. God will provide, but you need to make an act of the will or change of heart to align your will and heart with God's will.

Meditation VIII

On Loneliness, Family and Community

Time: 50 minutes

Position: Easy pose, sitting with legs crossed (Indian style); support your back against a wall if needed. Substitute other comfortable sitting positions with your back straight. Try kneeling with your buttocks resting on your heels.

Environment: Light a candle. Place it four feet in front of you on the floor or on a candleholder at eye level. If in community, put the candle in the center of the group. Check a watch.

Meditation: Begin with one Hail Mary prayed out loud, whether you are alone or in a group. Silently pray three decades of the rosary and coordinate each Hail Mary with your breath. Choose to change your position, *asana*, with each decade of the rosary. After thirty Hail Marys, silently become conscious of God's presence and begin a conversation with Jesus, talking to him about loneliness, community, and family. Observe your thoughts and the people in your life. How can you love more? Mother Teresa said that the greatest disease of our time is not leprosy or tuberculosis, but feeling unwanted. Can you love someone who is unwanted? Do you love yourself? Do you love God? Talk with God. If you feel you are distracted from your conversation with God, refocus by silently praying one or two Hail Marys, coordinating the words with your breathing. After thirty minutes, thank God for the gift of love.

Change your seated position if necessary. Pray the final two decades of the rosary silently. Thank Mary and God. Conclude with one Hail Mary prayed out loud.

Act: "Do you want to do something beautiful for God? There is a person who needs you. This is your chance," says Mother Teresa. Love.

Meditation IX

On Nonattachment

Time: 60 minutes

Position: Easy pose, sitting with legs crossed (Indian style); support your back against a wall if needed. Substitute other comfortable sitting positions with your back straight. Try three different yoga positions, changing position every twenty minutes.

Environment: Light a candle. Place it four feet in front of you on the floor or on a candleholder at eye level. If you are in a group, put the candle in the center of the group. Check a watch.

Meditation: Begin with one Hail Mary prayed out loud, whether you are alone or in a group. Silently pray three decades of the rosary and coordinate each Hail Mary with your breath. Choose to change your position, *asana*, with each decade of the rosary. After thirty Hail Marys, be conscious of God's presence. Be aware of what you need in life to accomplish your deepest desire, your God desire. Observe the things that are a part of your life that either assist or detract from your God desire. Feel the freedom of having fewer possessions and the extra time that is freed up when one has fewer possessions. Observe your thoughts. Repeat the following phrase silently, "Things do not matter, people matter."[14] Realize that your purpose on earth is to realize and fulfill your God desire, to the greater glory of God. Talk with God. If you feel you are distracted from your conversation with God, refocus by silently praying one or two Hail Marys, coordinating your breath with your prayers. After forty minutes, thank God for the gift of life. Change your seated position if necessary. Pray two more decades of the rosary silently. Thank Mary and God. Conclude with one Hail Mary prayed out loud.

Meditation X

Breathing Peace into the Universe:
A Prayer of Peace against World War.

Time: 60 minutes

Position: Easy pose, sitting with legs crossed (Indian style); support your back against a wall if needed. Substitute other comfortable sitting positions with your back straight. Try three different yoga positions. An alternative setting is to practice this meditation as a walking meditation. The three parts of the Hail Mary and the three parts of your breath should synchronize with a given foot. This is great exercise. Gandhi said that walking is the best and most natural form of exercise to keep the body fit (assuming good diet). A one-hour brisk walk was a part of Gandhi's daily routine. Adding the Hail Mary and *pranayama* breathing only increases the health benefits of this good habit. Be patient with yourself. Coordinating your breath to a given step and to the mental cadence of the Hail Mary takes practice. This meditation will greatly aid your endurance if you have to walk long distances without food or water.

Environment: Light a candle. Place it four feet in front of you on the floor or on a candleholder at eye level. If in community, put the candle in the center of the group. If you choose the alternative setting for this meditation, choose a path that will allow you to walk for one hour in God's presence. Check a watch.

Meditation: Begin with one Hail Mary prayed out loud, whether you are alone or in a group. Silently say three decades of the rosary and coordinate each Hail Mary with your breath. Try to coordinate your three-part breath with the three-part Hail Mary while walking, if you make this a walking meditation. In time you will naturally synchronize the parts of your breath and the Hail Mary with your walking. With each breath, breathe in God's grace. Feel the breath and grace of God being formed and created within you as you retain the breath.[15] While exhaling, be conscious of the grace that you are breathing into the universe. Feel the peace you are exhaling into the universe. You are answering Mary's plea at Fatima to pray the rosary and lead the world toward peace. Pope John Paul II also emphasized the rosary as a weapon of peace:

> By focusing our eyes on Christ, the Rosary also makes us peacemakers in the world. By its nature as an insistent choral petition in harmony with Christ's invitation to "pray ceaselessly" (Luke 18:1), the Rosary allows us to hope that, even today, the difficult "battle" for peace can be won.[16]

Silently pray five decades of the rosary (fifty Hail Marys). After praying five decades, spend the next half hour in silence talking with God and being conscious of his presence. If you feel you are distracted from your conversation with God, refocus by silently praying one or two Hail Marys, coordinating your breath with your prayer. After one hour, thank God for the gift of peace and the opportunity to be a peacemaker and cocreator. Thank Mary and God. Conclude with one Hail Mary prayed out loud.

Peace.

Glossary of Terms

Asana. Yoga position or posture of the body.

Ashram. A spiritual retreat and educational center.

Breviary. A Catholic book containing the hymns, prayers, and offices for the canonical hours.

Japa yoga. A type of yoga; mental repetitive prayer.

Mantra. A word or phrase repeated in meditation to bring an individual to a higher state of consciousness.

Prana. Life force, or energy, found in every particle of the universe.

Pranayama. The art of yoga breathing.

Swamiji. A term of respectful address for a swami or monk.

Yogi. A person who practices yoga.

Notes

1. *The Sivananda Companion to Yoga* is an excellent guide to the benefits of Yoga and the many postures, *asanas,* that are excellent for meditation. It was created by members of the Sivananda Yoga Center (see below).

2. The Sivananda Yoga Center, *The Sivananda Companion to Yoga: A Complete Guide to the Physical Postures, Breathing Exercises, Diet, Relaxation, and Meditation Techniques of Yoga* (New York: Fireside, 2000).

3. *Pranayama* means a technique designed to magnetize the spine and brain and give the practitioner mastery over the heart and senses. In *pranayama* the breath moves up and down the spine. On inhaling, the breath is imagined to move up the spine, until the attention is placed at the spot between the brows; then, on the exhale, the breath is imagined moving down the spine. To learn more about *pranayama,* visit The Pranayama Institute. Available from World Wide Web: http://www.pranayama. org/.

4. *The Sivananda Companion to Yoga.*

5. Ibid.

6. Mantras are words or phrases repeated in meditation to bring an individual to a higher state of consciousness.

7. Luciano Bernardi, Peter Sleight, Gabriele Bandinelli et al., "Beyond Science? Effect of rosary prayer and yoga mantras on autonomic cardiovascular rhythms: comparative study." *British Journal of Medicine* 323 (December 22-29, 2001), 1446-49.

8. *The New Catholic Encyclopedia.* 2nd ed., s.v. "Hail Mary."

9. Bernardi, 1447.

10. Alexis Carrel, *The Voyage to Lourdes* (New York: Harper and Brothers, 1950).

11. Malcolm Muggeridge, *Something Beautiful for God: Mother Teresa of Calcutta* (San Francisco: Harper-Collins, 1986).

12. The message from Mother Teresa can be found in *Rosary Meditations from Mother Teresa of Calcutta*, an updated version of *Loving Jesus with the Heart of Mary–Eucharistic Meditations on the Fifteen Mysteries of the Rosary*, by Martin Lucia, SS.CC. Published by and available from the Missionaries of the Blessed Sacrament, PO Box 1701, Plattsburgh, NY 12901. Also available online at http://www.acfp2000.com/.

13. *The New Catholic Encyclopedia,* supra.

14. A frequent saying of Father Patrick O'Neill, PhD, a priest who founded Catholic Volunteers in Florida in 1983 while he was president of St. Thomas University, Miami.

15. Exhaling into the universe and the changing of the breath within us was an idea of Cathy Kennedy, former opinion/spirituality editor of *The Florida Catholic.*

16. Pope John Paul II, *Apostolic Letter on the Rosary of the Virgin Mary (Rosarium Virginis Mariae).* October 16, 2002.

ILLUMINATIONBOOKS

Other Books in the Series

Little Pieces of Light...Darkness and Personal Growth
   by Joyce Rupp

Joy, The Dancing Spirit of Love Surrounding You
   by Beverly Elaine Eanes

Why Are You Worrying?
   by Joseph W. Ciarrocchi

Appreciating God's Creation Through Scripture
   by Alice L. Laffey

Let Yourself Be Loved
   by Phillip Bennett

A Rainy Afternoon with God
   by Catherine B. Cawley

Time, A Collection of Fragile Moments
   by Joan Monahan

15 Ways to Nourish Your Faith
   by Susan Shannon Davies

Following in the Footsteps of Jesus
   by Gerald D. Coleman, SS, and David M. Pettingill

God Lives Next Door
   by Lyle K. Weiss

Hear the Just Word & Live It
        by Walter J. Burghardt, SJ

The Love That Keeps Us Sane
        by Marc Foley, OCD

The Threefold Way of Saint Francis
        by Murray Bodo, OFM

Everyday Virtues
        by John W. Crossin, OSFS

The Mysteries of Light
        by Roland J. Faley, TOR

Healing Mysteries
        by Adrian Gibbons Koester

Carrying the Cross with Christ
        by Joseph T. Sullivan

Saintly Deacons
        by Deacon Owen F. Cumming

Finding God Today
        by E. Springs Steele